ALL ABOUT ME

Verses I Can Read

Selected by Leland B. Jacobs

Drawings by Hertha R. Depper

GARRARD PUBLISHING COMPANY
CHAMPAIGN, ILLINOIS

Acknowledgments

Child Life: For "The Wish" by Ann Friday from *Child Life,* Copyright 1955. Reprinted by permission of Child Life.

Doubleday & Company, Inc.: For "Singing-Time," copyright 1923 by George H. Doran Company, from *The Fairy Green* by Rose Fyleman. Reprinted by permission of Doubleday & Company, Inc.

E. P. Dutton & Co., Inc.: For "Out Walking" — 4 lines; and "Speed" — 8 lines from the book *Around and About* by Marchette Chute. Copyright © 1957 by E. P. Dutton & Co., Inc., publishers, and reprinted with their permission.

Aileen Fisher for permission to reprint "Snow Color" by Aileen Fisher.

Harcourt Brace Jovanovich, Inc.: For "It Tickles" from *Wide Awake and Other Poems,* © 1959 by Myra Cohn Livingston. Reprinted by permission of Harcourt Brace Jovanovich, Inc.

G. P. Putnam's Sons: For 'When I Was Lost," "Bad," and "Big," reprinted by permission of G. P. Putnam's Sons from *All Together* by Dorothy Aldis. Copyright 1925, 1926, 1927, 1928, 1934, 1939, 1952 by Dorothy Aldis. For "Little," reprinted by permission of G. P. Putnam's Sons from *Everything and Anything* by Dorothy Aldis. Copyright 1925, 1926, 1927, renewed 1953, 1954, 1955 by Dorothy Aldis.

Scott, Foresman and Company: For "After a Bath" from *Up the Windy Hill* by Aileen Fisher. Reprinted by permission of Scott, Foresman and Company.

The Viking Press, Inc.: For "Purple Patches" by Tom Robinson (10 lines) from *In and Out* by Tom Robinson. Copyright 1943 by Tom Robinson, copyright © renewed 1971 by Donald F. Robinson, Jack F. Robinson & Lincoln F. Robinson. Reprinted by permission of The Viking Press, Inc.

Henry Z. Walck, Inc.: For "My Raincoat" and "What! No Ideas?" from *The Life I Live* by Lois Lenski. Copyright 1965 by Lois Lenski. Published by Henry Z. Walck, Inc. Used by permission of the author.

Western Publishing Company, Inc.: For "Mountain Climbers" and "To the Barber's Shop" from *The Golden Book of 365 Stories* by Kathryn Jackson. Copyright 1955 Western Publishing Company, Inc. Used by permission of Golden Press.

ALL ABOUT ME
Verses I Can Read

My Growing

In the Mirror

In the mirror
I can see
that I'm
not one,
but I am
three.
The mirror
is the place
to see
I,
  Myself,
    And Me.

Merlin Millet

Big

Now I can catch and throw a ball
And spell
Cat. Dog.
And Pig,
I have finished being small
And started
Being Big.

Dorothy Aldis

Something about Me

There's something about me
   That I'm knowing.
There's something about me
   That isn't showing.

   I'm growing!

Unknown

My Doings

My Drawings

I drew my mother's picture,
  Another of my dad.
They told me that my pictures are
  The best they ever had.
They even showed them to their friends,
  And everyone was glad.

B. J. Lee

What I Drew

I drew a house,
I drew a tree,
I drew a sky,
And I drew me.

I drew a cat.
I drew a yard.
I drew it all.
It wasn't hard.

Lee Blair

Little

I am the sister of him
And he is my brother.
He is too little for us
To talk to each other.

So every morning I show him
My doll and my book;
And every morning he still is
Too little to look.

Dorothy Aldis

Wonderful Dinner

I set the table
I made it all neat,
And everyone said
When they sat down to eat,
"The table looks pretty.
You did it just right."

It was a wonderful
Dinner that night!

Speed

Do you have to go
   So very fast?
They say to me
   As I go past.
But I must go fast.
   Unless I do
I can't get where
   I'm going to.

Marchette Chute

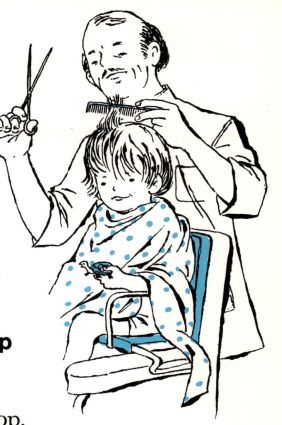

To the Barber's Shop

Once a month
With a hop, hop, hop,
Off I go
To the barber's shop.

Once a month
With a snip, snip, snip
He cuts my hair
And home I skip.

Kathryn Jackson

Who Went There?

Who went there?
See the tracks in the snow.

Who went there?
Doesn't anyone know?

Who went there?
There are tracks. Do you see?

Who went there?
Yes! Yes! It was ME! . . .

Anonymous

Out Walking

I carry bits of bread along
    And bits of bacon-ends,
Because a person never knows
    When he will meet his friends.

Marchette Chute

To the Store

Where have you been?
Where have you been?

I've been to the store.
I just got in.

Where did you go?
Where did you go?

I went to the store.
I told you so.

What did you get?
What did you get?

What I got
I can't tell yet.

Anonymous

What! No Ideas?

Do, do, what shall I do?
What shall I do
the whole day through?

Go, go, where shall I go?
That's just what
I'd like to know!

Play, play, what shall I play?
When all my friends
have gone away?

Lois Lenski

My Wishes

The Wish

Each birthday wish
I've ever made
Really does come true.
Each year I wish
I'll grow some more
And every year
I do!

Ann Friday

18

Washing Time Wish

At washing time
  I always wish
That I could wash
  Like fish.

Unknown

Star Light, Star Bright

Star light, star bright,
First star I see tonight,
I wish I may,
I wish I might
Have the wish I wish tonight.

Old Rhyme

Away Up High

If I could fly
Up to the sky,
Up to the sky so far,
I think that I
Would like it high
On a bright and shining star.

Unknown

Mountain Climbers

We piled a pillow mountain up,
And I climbed to the top.
But then I slipped —
I wish we'd fixed
A softer place to stop!

Kathryn Jackson

My Raincoat

It's raining, it's raining,
　But I do not care,
I have a new raincoat
　That I want to wear.
I have a new raincoat
　It came from the store,
I want it to sprinkle,
　I want it to pour.

Lois Lenski

Wet

The clouds were dark,
The thunder crashed,
And I began to run.
The rain came pouring
Down on me
And I was wet! What fun!

Anonymous

Bad

I've been bad and I'm in bed
For the naughty things I said.

I'm in bed. I wish I had
Not said those things that were so bad.

I wish that I'd been good instead.
But I was bad. And I'm in bed.

Dorothy Aldis

My Toolbox

My toolbox is a wishing box.
  I make a wish or two,
Then open it and take some tools
  And make my wish come true.

Unknown

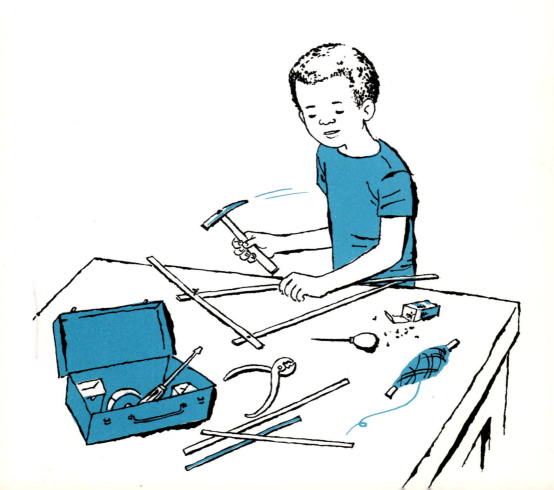

My Moods

When I'm Angry

When I'm angry,
  I can yell.
People hear me
  Very well.

When I'm angry,
  I can roar.
People hear me
  Way next door.

B. J. Lee

Singing-Time

I wake in the morning early
And always, the very first thing,
I poke out my head and I sit up in bed
And I sing and I sing and I sing.

Rose Fyleman

Sun — Moon — Stars

I see the sun.
   The sun sees me.
We beam on each other.
   Happy are we.

I see the moon.
   The moon sees me.
We look at each other.
   Happy are we.

I see the stars.
   The stars see me.
We wink at each other.
   Happy are we.

Unknown

Glad

Oh, I can sing,
And I can walk,
And I can skip,
And I can talk,
And I can skate
And climb a tree.
How glad I am
That I am me!

Lee Blair

When I Was Lost

Underneath my belt
My stomach was a stone.
Sinking was the way I felt.
And hollow.
And alone.

Dorothy Aldis

My Thoughts

Snow Color

I used to think
that snow was white.
And then,
I saw it blue one night.

And then,
I saw it gold one day,
with purple shadows
and with gray.

And then,
one morning it was pink.
So now
I don't know what to think.

Aileen Fisher

Purple Patches

Purple patches all around,
In the trees and on the ground.
Everywhere I look I see
Purple patches seeing me.
And I wonder then if I
Have purple patches in my eye?

Tom Robinson

The Purple Cow

I never saw a purple cow,
  I never hope to see one.
But this I will say anyhow,
  I'd rather see than be one.

Gelett Burgess

Whistle

I whistle
   in the morning.
I whistle
   when it's noon.
I whistle
   in the sunshine.
I whistle
   to the moon.
I whistle,
   whistle,
   whistle.
Do you like
   my whistle tune?

B. J. Lee

It Tickles

It tickles
  when I brush
  my teeth.

Not on top,
But underneath.

Myra Cohn Livingston

After a Bath

After my bath
I try, try, try
to wipe myself
till I'm dry, dry, dry.

Hands to wipe
and fingers and toes
and two wet legs
and a shiny nose.

Just think how much
less time I'd take
if I were a dog
and could shake, shake, shake.

Aileen Fisher

Bed Time

Dinner's over;
   Lights are lit.
How I hate
   To think of it,
But clocks and stars
   And a full, round moon
All say that bed time's
   Coming soon.

Jay Lee